SHAKERS
RE-STIRRED

SHAKERS

RE-STIRRED

by John Godber and Jane Thornton

JOSEF WEINBERGER PLAYS

LONDON

First published in 1987
by Josef Weinberger Ltd (pka Warner/Chappell Plays Ltd)
12-14 Mortimer Street, London, W1T 3JJ

This edition first published 1993
Reprinted 1997, 2000

ISBN 0 85676 166 4

SHAKERS was first presented by the Hull Truck Theatre
Company at the Spring Street Theatre, Hull, on 29 January,
1984, with the following cast:

ADELE	Alison Grant
CAROL	Alison Watt
MEL	Marion Summerfield
NICKY	Sherry Baines

Directed by John Godber

SHAKERS RE-STIRRED was first presented by the Hull Truck
Theatre Company in 1991, with the following cast:

ADELE	Nicola Vickery
CAROL	Joanne Wootton
MEL	Tracy Sweetinburgh
NICKY	Rebecca Clay

Directed by John Godber

Designed by Liam Doona

photograph by Tony Baines from the Hull Truck Theatre Company production of Shakers

ACT ONE

*A modern cafe bar, post-modernist structure, which is
essentially an open space. Four chairs are the only real
furniture. Four girls are dressed in the height of fashion.
They are waitresses. Lights rise. They stand centre stage and
are lit by spotlight.*

ADELE   Ladies and gentlemen welcome to *Shakers*. That
        trendy bar in the main street where the neon light
        shines out into the night tempting passers-by. That
        place where dreams come true. Where time stands
        still, where everyone wants to be seen, from the
        checkout girls to the chinless yuppies . . .

CAROL   Where *pied a terre* has replaced Hush Puppies.
        Where the plastic world has taken root,
        And the social climber counts his loot . . .

MEL   We stand and serve, we grin and smile,
        We serve to please, and all the while
        We do, we burn up deep inside
        With all the pain we're meant to hide.

NICKY   And though at times we'd like to scream,
        It wouldn't wake you from your dream
        Of *Long Tall Ice* and deep-freeze beer.
        We see you glance, we know you leer . . .

ADELE   And secretly you long to touch us as we pass.
        And rub your hands across our arse,
        And wink and smile and glow with lust.
        We work this bar that is worse than hell.

CAROL   We are Carol.

ADELE   Adele.

NICKY   Nicky.

MEL   And Mel.

ADELE   We pull the drinks,
We take your bile,
We serve the food . . .

MEL   We have to smile
No matter how crude or rude you care to be.

CAROL   No matter what you do . . .

NICKY   No matter what you say . . .

ADELE   There's a happy smiling face that comes your way.

(Lights up, we are in "real" mode. The girls clean. The bar is about to open. CAROL addresses the audience.)

CAROL   I'm sorry we're closed, you'll have to come back later. Sorry.

MEL   Time is it?

NICKY   'Quarter to.

MEL   Another day another dollar . . .

CAROL   Closed, read the sign.

MEL   If you can read.

NICKY   Happy hour doesn't start till seven. That's when all the fun starts.

CAROL   Yippee!

NICKY   Happy hour, seven till ten.

MEL   It's a long hour.

NICKY   And not very happy.

ADELE   . . . It can be desperate.

NICKY   That'd make a change, 'desperate hour' seven till eleven, bring your own Valium.

CAROL   Some of the people we get in here you need it.

ADELE   Valium?

MEL   (*to audience*) We are closed, come back in ten minutes, we're having a chat so knob off!

ADELE   A true professional at work.

CAROL   Charming.

MEL   That's how to deal with 'em. They think we're shit, I think they're shit I don't take any prisoners.

NICKY   No . . . they'd rather kill themselves I'll bet.

CAROL   I just ignore the awkward ones.

ADELE   Sensible.

MEL   Well you must ignore everybody in that case Carol, you must be the only waitresses in here who doesn't serve anybody. They're all a set of bastards.

CAROL   Thank you Desmond Morris.

NICKY   Who?

MEL   This is the real world, Carol.

CAROL   Don't start that again.

MEL   This is the real world, mad bad and ugly.

NICKY   Like you . . .

MEL   Go and die Nicky, okay.

CAROL   This is the real world is it?

ADELE   'Fraid so.

MEL   What time did you get in Adele? I didn't notice.

ADELE   You what?

MEL   What time did you get in?

ADELE   When?

MEL   Tonight.

ADELE   Why?

MEL   I just wondered.

ADELE   Listen Mel I'm here, that's the important thing.

NICKY   True enough.

ADELE   I'll never let you down, that's the important thing.

CAROL   Go on then Mel.

MEL   What?

CAROL   I thought you were going to tell us something.

MEL   Who?

CAROL   You. You couldn't contain yourself about half an hour ago and now you've gone all shy on us.

NICKY   That's not like you.

MEL   Oh it is, I'm very shy and retiring I am. All the family are.

CAROL   Do you mean there's more like you?

ADELE   Go on then.

MEL   What?

NICKY   Tell us . . .

MEL   He's asked me.

CAROL   Who?

MEL   Steve.

NICKY   You hardly know him.

ADELE   I thought it was Paul?

NICKY   That was last month.

MEL   Ha ha.

CAROL   So it's the real thing?

ADELE   So is Coke.

NICKY   But it rots your teeth.

MEL   At least I've got a bloke Carol . . . ?

CAROL   Yeh . . . lucky you.

NICKY   Will it last though, that's what we all want to know?

MEL   I hope.

NICKY   How long have you known him?

MEL   Long enough.

ADELE   How long is that?

MEL   How long do you want it to be?

NICKY   Oooohhhh.

MEL   What's up Adele, are you jealous?

ADELE   Yeh jealous to death.

MEL   I bet you are and all.

NICKY   What's happened to Paul then? He looked nice. He'd be alright for me. I like spotty men.

MEL   I think Paul fancied Adele actually.

ADELE   I'm flattered. *Down Stage*

MEL   But I think he got scared off.

NICKY   But not as frightening as Paul, I should know I saw him in the daylight.

CAROL   He wasn't that bad.

MEL   Yes he was.

ADELE   When's the big day Mel?

MEL   Soon.

NICKY   Is it going to be in Peach . . . or Lemon?

MEL   Lemon I think. You'll all get an invite. And you can bring a man each. If you can find one.

NICKY   You could have Emma as a bridesmaid?

ADELE   I don't think so.

MEL   Where do you leave her?

ADELE   I usually leave her with my Mum. But my Mum's ill. So I've left her with Craig's Mum, tonight.

MEL   Oh right.

ADELE   Congratulations.

MEL   Thanks.

ADELE   I hope you're as happy as I thought I was going to be.

MEL   I'm sure I will be.

NICKY   I wish I could find the real thing in my life.

CAROL   Why?

NICKY   All the men I meet are like cartoon characters.

ADELE   There are plenty of fish in the sea.

NICKY   That's what I thought.

MEL   Yeh but she's not looking for a fish are you?

NICKY   I don't know what I'm looking for. All that can wait anyway, I've had some good news today, so the world is my oyster.

CAROL   Speaking of which . . .

ADELE   The seafood pasta is back on. *Get up*

CAROL   There's a taste of class . . .

NICKY   In a highball glass. Cocktails on ice.

MEL   You want a lemon slice?

ADELE   Or a *Piña Colada*? *Up to bar*

CAROL   Or a *Vodka Hula*?

NICKY   *Tequila Sunrise*?

MEL   Or a *Southern Gin Cooler*?

CAROL   It looks exciting.

MEL   It looks a scream.

ADELE   But you pay through the nose, when your head's in a dream.

         (*They move to next positions.* NICKY *and* CAROL *become two punters,* DAZ *and* TREV.)

NICKY   Daz.

CAROL   And Trev . . .

ADELE   Hard as nails . . .

CAROL   They shop at Next . . .

MEL   And have been in jail . . .

CAROL   They're out on the town . . .

ADELE   They're after the skirt . . .

CAROL   It's fifteen below . . .

NICKY   It's freezing out there . . . but these lads are hard.

MEL   They don't give a toss.

NICKY   They've got muscles like knots, in dental floss . . .
they're Daz . . .

CAROL   And they're Trev . . .

NICKY   They've come down to the bar . . .

CAROL   To get themselves a bev . . .

NICKY   Go on then Trev ask her.

CAROL   You ask her.

NICKY   What's wrong are you scared? Chicken shit.

CAROL   I don't want a farty cocktail anyway, I'd rather have
a pint.

NICKY   It'll be a laugh, see her face.

CAROL   Okay, which one are you going to ask?

NICKY   The one with the tits, not that other one, she's too
skinny.

CAROL   Yeh that big one's alright.

NICKY   Yeh not many of them to a pound.

CAROL   You're well hard.

NICKY   Too right.

CAROL   How much are they?

NICKY   I don't think they're for sale.

CAROL   I meant the drinks dickhead.

NICKY   About two quid, I think.

CAROL   It's not worth it.

NICKY   Course it is, for a laugh.

CAROL   Loads of blokes'll ask her for it, I bet she doesn't bat an eyelid.

NICKY   Yes but are they good looking?

CAROL   Like you, you mean?

NICKY   You said it mate.

CAROL   Look out she's coming over.

NICKY   Brilliant.

(MEL *arrives to serve them.*)

MEL   Are you being served?

CAROL   No we're not.

MEL   Can I help you?

CAROL   Yes, he wants one of them cocktails.

MEL   Which one do you fancy?

NICKY   They both look alright to me darling. No offence.

(*They both laugh.*)

CAROL   Excuse my friend, he doesn't know how to behave in front of ladies.

MEL   Really?

CAROL   Yes.

MEL   I had noticed.

NICKY   I want a *Long Slow Comfortable Screw*. So how about that?

MEL   What a surprise. Regular or giant-sized?

NICKY   You what?

MEL   Large or small?

NICKY   Don't get personal.

CAROL   You guess love.

NICKY   Make a wish. (*They laugh.*)

CAROL   Sorry love just a joke.

MEL   Oh, is that what it was?

NICKY   Yeah, funny eh?

MEL   Very.

CAROL   Don't smile much do you?

NICKY   Too much bed, not enough sleep, eh?

MEL   Look do you want a drink or not, I haven't got all night.

NICKY   How much are they?

MEL   Three quid for a small one seven quid for a large one.

NICKY   What a rip off.

CAROL   Expensive in't it?

MEL   You don't have to have one.

NICKY   Don't get touchy.

MEL   I'm waiting.

CAROL   She's waiting.

NICKY   I'll have a small one.

CAROL   And me.

MEL   With or without ice?

BOTH   Erm, with ice . . .

Stay by bar

MEL Bleeding cocktails, it's the same every night. You always get a couple of uptown *Zombies* with a *Glad Eye* doing a *Pick Me Up*, sometimes promising a holiday with a *Tequila Sunrise* on *Montego Bay*, hoping for a ride on his *Piña Colada*. What he really wants is a *Long Slow Comfortable Screw, Between the Sheets* in his *Side Car*. I'd just like to give the *Bosom Caresser* a *Sparkling Punch* in his *Dicki Dicki*, so he falls *Head over Heels* and goes home clutching his *Blue Bols*. Six Pounds please.

(The actresses pick up the serving rhythm and move around the stage.)

CAROL You want a *Piña Colada*?

NICKY Or a *Vodka Hula*?

CAROL *Tequila Sunrise*?

MEL Or a *Southern Gin Cooler*?

ADELE What ever you ask for we can make. Just give us a name and we'll give you a shake.

MEL I've just served two right prats.

ADELE What's new?

MEL Not a lot actually.

ADELE We can have a breather before the rush starts. I hate Fridays.

MEL And Mondays, Tuesdays, Wednesdays.

ADELE *(to* MEL*)* You're really funny.

NICKY I don't mind Fridays. I mean at least it's busy and you don't have to stand about like a spare part. I like it like that, makes it seem more worthwhile.

CAROL And Mario gets more value for money.

NICKY And the time passes quicker. It's better than doing nothing.

MEL   Is it?

NICKY   I think it is.

MEL   I'd rather do nothing. You get paid the same. We
          could sit at the bar all night put the stereo on, have
          a chat . . . that'd be great.

ADELE   I don't think I'd bother coming.

MEL   I'm not saying anything Adele.

ADELE   Razor sharp tonight aren't you?

NICKY   My feet are killing me already.

ADELE   So who have we got in tonight?

MEL   I'm surprised you're even interested.

CAROL   There's a theatre booking. And a twenty-first
          birthday party coming in at nine.

MEL   Oh nice, all streamers and funny hats?

CAROL   And the usual crowd.

NICKY   Oh don't be like that Mel, they've probably been
          looking forward to this all day.

          (*Music, "The Girl from Ipenema". MEL, NICKY,
          CAROL and ADELE become SUSAN, ELAINE, SHARON
          and TRACEY, respectively. They all work at the
          supermarket and are set at the checkout tills. It's
          quiet in terms of customers. [This is not necessarily
          an up-market supermarket.] Muzak plays.*)

ALL   "Supermarket."

NICKY   Check for fifty. (*Pounds.*)

MEL   Susan.

NICKY   Elaine; twenty-one and should be celebrating.

ALL   Yehhhhhh . . . (*A cheer that tails off.*)

CAROL   Tracey.

ADELE   Sharon.

NICKY   God it's dragging.

MEL   I'm bored.

ADELE   I'm vegetating . . .

CAROL   I hate it on the tills, me. In the last half hour all
I've had is an old woman with some organic
tomatoes.

ADELE   It's always the same this time of day.

MEL   Yeah, boring.

CAROL   I was supposed to be on the shop floor today doing
cereals, but they've put that bloody student on, it
makes me sick.

NICKY   It's not fair is it?

CAROL   I mean, she's only here for the holidays. I don't like
her.

ADELE   No, I don't.

CAROL   I wouldn't care but I was loading bloody freezers all
day yesterday, my hands nearly dropped off it was
that cold.

MEL   They should give you gloves you know. You're not
supposed to do it without gloves.

CAROL   I know.

MEL   But they don't care.

CAROL   No. (*Pause.*)

NICKY   What a birthday . . .

ADELE   Never mind.

NICKY   I can't wait for tonight.

MEL   Yeh, at least that's something to look forward to.

CAROL   I can't believe you're twenty-one . . .

NICKY   Well I am . . .

CAROL   But it seems so old.

ADELE   It's not exactly middle aged. You've got your whole life ahead.

NICKY   Yeh, and I'll tell you what I might pack it in here, I might do that hairdressing course at tech that our Sandra's doing. She says it's great.

CAROL   You wouldn't have as much money though would you?

NICKY   Who's bothered? I've always fancied hairdressing, and it's got to be better than this.

CAROL   I suppose so.

NICKY   Our Sandra's doing my hair for when we go out.

ADELE   Oh yes?

NICKY   French plait.

MEL   Oh.

ADELE   What are you wearing?

MEL   That black dress again I suppose.

CAROL   It's nice that.

MEL   It's alright.

NICKY   Me, Shaz and Trace are off shopping at dinner time for some new stuff.

MEL   God . . .

NICKY   Well it is my twenty-first.

ADELE   You can come if you want.

MEL   I can't, I've got no money.

ADELE   There's a sale on.

MEL   Oh go on then . . .

CAROL   We need something smart, it's posh that *Shakers* place you know.

NICKY   Now that's something I wouldn't mind.

ALL   What?

NICKY   Working in a cocktail bar!

        (*Music to take us back into Shakers. The girls become the waitresses. They meet around centre stage.*)

        I think I've got a corn.

ADELE   Yeh table four. The man with the horse teeth and the B. O.

CAROL   That's right. Sweet corn, two tagliatelle's and a bottle of house red.

NICKY   No, on my foot.

CAROL   Stop wingeing.

MEL   Have you seen that bloke with the nose and the glasses?

NICKY   Have I? He's been dying to ask me for a *Slow Screw*, I can see him looking at it on the menu, then he comes to the bar all determined, and he chickens out and asks for *Aqua Libra* and some peanuts.

CAROL   Good job by the looks of him.

NICKY   I can't understand it, he still blushes.

ADELE   He looks nice.

MEL   Well with them peanuts and that chili pizza he'll pebble-dash the toilets.

NICKY   Ugh, Mel.

MEL   Well he will. Pebble-dash man, or what?

ADELE   As long as we don't have to clear it away.

MEL   Are you coming tomorrow Adele?

ADELE   Why?

MEL   Just asking that's all . . .

ADELE   Don't worry Mel.

MEL   It's just that it's not fair on us, we have to set up. I mean we haven't told Mario you were late.

ADELE   Yet?

         (*The four actresses react to the last line with a loud guffaw of laughter. They have instantly become businessmen.*)

MEL   A table for three love, a table for three.

NICKY   Here we go . . .

MEL   No it's all right we'll stand at the bar.

NICKY   Certainly.

MEL   Is that alright, Gerry? Mervyn?

CAROL   Gerry . . .

ADELE   Mervyn . . .

MEL   Yes that's tickety boo . . . Stand at the bar, prevent anyone else being served . . .

         (*A guffaw of laughter from the businessmen.*)

NICKY	Can I get you a drink? It's Happy Hour at the moment. double measures for the price of one.
MEL	Amazing.
CAROL	Absolutely.
ADELE	Of course.
MEL	What do you have?
NICKY	What would you like, sir?
MEL	Too early for any of that thank you.
CAROL	Speak for yourself.
MEL	I was. (*A loud laugh.*)
NICKY	Sorry.
MEL	You would be . . .
NICKY	You wait for hours until the fat oaf has decided what he wants. Then, after adjusting his trousers several times, he'll go for the lager.
MEL	I'll have a lager.
NICKY	Then he'll suddenly change his mind, because of his blood pressure.
MEL	No no no . . . must think about the old blood pressure.
NICKY	And you nod, like you're concerned.
MEL	I think I'll have . . .
NICKY	He'll go for the Martini.
MEL	Martini.
NICKY	Knew it. With lemonade and ice.
MEL	With . . .

NICKY   Lemonade and ice, sir?

MEL   How marvellous. What's everyone else having,
         Gerry? Mervyn? What's your poison?

NICKY   They've just been looking at a new car outside.

ADELE   We've just been looking at a new car outside.

MEL   What're you having?

ADELE   Martini.

CAROL   And me, Willy.

MEL   Three Martini's lovey . . .

NICKY   I wince and smile . . . and serve . . .

         (*They take the drinks and down the hatch. It takes
         their breath.*)

CAROL   Wonderful.

MEL   Excellent.

ADELE   Didn't even touch the sides.

MEL   Same again Gerry? Mervyn?

CAROL   Gerry.

ADELE   Mervyn.

CAROL   Oh I don't know.

ADELE   I have a hell of a drive.

CAROL   Oh what the hell . . .

NICKY   And four doubles later the laughter starts . . . (*All
         laugh loud and hard.*)

ADELE   This man goes into a butchers, and he says to the
         butcher. "Have you got a sheep's head?" And the
         butcher says, "No, it's just the way I comb my
         hair."

MEL   Bloody hell, that's bloody funny . . .

CAROL   I say Willy, what are you driving at the moment?

MEL   Me . . . a car . . . (*All guffaw.*) No but seriously I'm
           driving the new Sierra.

CAROL   Really, how do you find it?

MEL   Well I just open the garage door and there it is . . .

CAROL   Nice girl . . . the waitress, nice legs.

ADELE   Yes she reminds me of Jackie at the office.

MEL   Which one's Jackie?

ADELE   Tall brunette with the dirty mouth.

MEL   Oh yes rather. Whenever she comes into my office I
           ask her to take something down.

CAROL   . . . But she never does . . .

MEL   Well she hasn't done yet. (*Laughter.*)

ADELE   Aren't they awkward on the road?

MEL   More awkward in the cupboard.

ADELE   I meant the Sierra, mores the pity.

MEL   No no, they're fine.

ADELE   I'm still with the old Rover.

CAROL   Yes, how is Vicky, Willy?

MEL   Shit Vicky, must ring the old girl . . . (*Phones.*)
           Hello Vicky, it's Willy. Hello darling how are you?
           Really? So sorry. Look, I know we're meeting
           Glenys and Clive but I'm afraid I'm still at the
           office, yes, something's come up . . . I'll try to get
           back later darling. But it's hell here at the moment
           . . . Love you, bye. Vicky is just the most amazing
           woman in the world.

CAROL	Does she know about you and . . .
MEL	Of course not. Anyway me and Becky are only having a bit of fun. She's married as well, her husband is in accounts.
ADELE	Bloody hell Willy, a bit near home.
CAROL	Oh look at the pissing time chaps, another drink whilst it's reasonable?
ADELE	I'd say the same again . . .
MEL	Cigar?
ALL	Cheers.
MEL	I say, would anyone care to eat?
ADELE	But what about Vicky's meal?
MEL	Oh it'll keep. Have you tasted Vicky's food? It's like bloody rubber.
CAROL	Well I could deal with a snack.
MEL	I say . . . lovey, can we have a table for three, we've decided we'd like to eat.
NICKY	Certainly sir, where would you like to sit?
MEL	On your face . . . (*A loud guffaw.*)
NICKY	Your table is ready, sir . . .
MEL	I'm sorry?
NICKY	Your table is ready . . . Fatty.
MEL	Excellent. Another drink anyone . . .
CAROL	Gerry?
ADELE	Mervyn?
MEL	And can we have the wine list?

NICKY   Of course . . . you silly old farts. (*They become the girls.*)

MEL   There's an arse-pincher. Table ten, by the bogs.

ADELE   Lucky you.

MEL   Just be aware.

CAROL   They should be locked up.

NICKY   The fat bloke on table six is having an affair and his wife can't cook.

ADELE   That's why he's having the affair.

MEL   Well have a good look at the arse-pincher on ten, I'm sure he's wearing a wig . . .

         (*The girls are serving imaginary characters, calling orders and receiving orders in turn, and also commenting on the evening so far.*)

CAROL   One minestrone.

NICKY   One onion soup?

ADELE   It's full already.

CAROL   Packed.

ADELE   Seafood pasta?

MEL   That is definitely a wig. He's bald as a bastard.

NICKY   It's not a wig . . . Anyone order the garlic bread?

ADELE   Put the air-conditioning on.

MEL   It's knackered.

ADELE   Great stuff. It is, it's a wig.

CAROL   One minestrone?

NICKY   It's like being on a tube.

CAROL   Excuse me, coming through.

ADELE   Sorry?

MEL   Well why don't you move then? Thank you Adele I
           told you it was. I can spot 'em a mile off.

ADELE   Anyone ordered seafood pasta?

NICKY   Oh God these shoes?

CAROL   What?

NICKY   Can you hear me?

ADELE   THE MUSIC IS TOO LOUD.

CAROL   You what?

NICKY   Shout up?

CAROL   (*shouts*) Is it a wig? Or what?

NICKY   What about that, he's not going back to his wife,
           he's going to meet Becky. It's all go.

CAROL   Onion soup?

ADELE   Prawn cocktail?

MEL   Sweetcorn?

NICKY   Excuse me, coming through, mind your backs
           please. Gerry's going to cover for him.

CAROL   Mind the doors.

ADELE   Mind the yuppies.

NICKY   Mind the liars.

           (ADELE *steps centre. This allows the others to peel
           away and set up the next tableaux.*)

ADELE   It's like a madhouse, cocktails then food, food then
           cocktails, I don't know if I'm coming or going. I

don't know my *Tom Collins* from my Bolognese.
Craig's mum's great she is, but I don't like leaving
my little girl with her . . . I mean tonight . . . I don't
know my head from my arse. I nearly had a stroke
getting here, I was charging down the street like
somebody not right.

(NICKY *has become a yuppie woman*, MEL *and* CAROL
serve upstage in a freeze.)

NICKY   Excuse me, you?

ADELE   Me?

NICKY   Yes.

ADELE   Oh God here we go.

NICKY   I'll take a mineral water with a lemon twist.

ADELE   Of course.

NICKY   With ice . . .

ADELE   (*to audience*) She obviously thinks I'm a dog.
Bastard.

NICKY   Sorry?

ADELE   Badoit?

NICKY   Evian.

ADELE   Woof woof . . .

(As ADELE *crosses the stage*, CAROL, *as a yuppie
man, grabs and fondles her arse. It's almost erotic.*)

Get off.

CAROL   What's wrong . . . I was just trying to get past you.

NICKY   I saw that Carl, you bastard . . .

CAROL   Vicky they love it, it's what they look forward to,
someone to brighten up the evening for them. Marry
me . . . marry me . . .

NICKY   Never . . . (*She breaks away from the scene and explains briefly to the audience.*) I don't need to, I'm young, a successful interior designer, I have toe-capped shoes and a mobile phone, I was educated at a top people's finishing school, and I also have a beautiful daughter with whom I can afford to spend quality time . . .

CAROL   Vicky you are an amazing woman.

NICKY   And a very rich father in the City.

CAROL   I love the City.

               (MEL *becomes an outraged punter. Screaming, shouting at* ADELE.)

MEL   You you you . . .

CAROL   (CARL) Can I make an order?

MEL   You . . . you.

ADELE   Me?

MEL   I haven't had my soup.

ADELE   It's on its way.

NICKY   Where's my Evian . . .

CAROL   Can I make an order now . . . ?

MEL   Am I going to get served in here tonight or not?

ADELE   It's on its way.

MEL   We should have gone to *Alexander's* . . .

NICKY   You.

CAROL   You.

NICKY   Oh come on . . .

CAROL   Can we have some pissing service . . .

NICKY   This is ridiculous.

(*A slow motion sequence.* ADELE *is bringing* NICKY *her drink, she slips on the floor. The drink flies into the air and then spills all over* NICKY *and* CAROL [CARL]).

NICKY   Oh oh oh my God, oh my God . . .

ADELE   Oh sorry sorry . . . I'm . . .

NICKY   This cost me six hundred pounds at Katherine Hamnet.

ADELE   Sorry Katherine. Sorry.

NICKY   Seafood pasta.

(*The waitresses are involved in chaotic serving.*)

MEL   Did you do that on purpose?

ADELE   . . . No it was an accident.

MEL   You bloody liar . . .

NICKY   Seafood pasta?

CAROL   I'm sure you ordered sirloin.

ADELE   . . . Another Lambrusco.

MEL   Another round of garlic mushrooms?

NICKY   (*shouts*) Has any one ordered seafood bloody pasta?

ADELE   (*a punter*) Do you have any black pepper?

MEL   Excuse me this wine is corked.

ADELE   This lager is off.

NICKY   One seafood pasta going back into the sea.

CAROL   I'm coming through watch your backs please.

MEL   (*a punter*) This wine is corked.

ADELE   Would madam like a kick in the teeth now or would
         she prefer it with her liqueur?

         (NICKY *downstage, with the others acting as chorus.*
         NB: [ALL] *denotes all except* NICKY.)

NICKY   At eight o'clock the theatre lot have gone to watch
         the curtain up.

CAROL   The mobile phones are up and off, and the power
         dressers disappear, talking of their business stresses.

ADELE   And it must be said there's no respite,
         This time of night, from the obtuse abuse,
         From the suited bods, the boring sods.

MEL   And they're here too, the local hacks,
         And the yuppies with their Filofax,
         Who pinch your arse and laugh.

ALL   Ha ha.

MEL   They all have their tale to tell,
         Arse-pinching yuppies who come from hell.

CAROL   And at this time the tips are few
         And the basic manners, too.

         (ADELE *breaks into a loud-mouthed man.*)

ADELE   Excuse me, am I going to have sit here and eat this
         rancid sirloin with my blessed fingers?

CAROL   Sorry sir. It's on its way.

ADELE   I should think so, I'll never eat in here again. And
         furthermore I'll recommend to all my very
         influential, and red-faced friends that they avoid the
         place like the plague. Stupid girl.

CAROL   I'm not stupid. (*All four become waitresses.*)

MEL   Mario's sent him a bottle of champagne.

NICKY   Greasy bastard.

CAROL   That's calmed him down.

ADELE   Yeh I know, he's even left a tip.

CAROL   How much?

MEL   Nosey.

ADELE   And off into the night he farts, a big, bloated
          balloon of Beaujolais, following his stomach the
          way a navvy follows a wheelbarrow.

NICKY   Having left a pound coin he feels sexy about
          himself.

ADELE   Goodnight, sir.

MEL   Don't Adele. I hate men . . . like that.

ADELE   He disappears into the night, a large Sierra, a
          magistrate.

CAROL   Ignorant bastard.

NICKY   Carol?

ADELE   He might have problems at home.

MEL   Yeh I bet.

CAROL   (*the lights begin to fade to a spotlight on* CAROL) I
          can't help it, I hate it when people just assume that
          because you do a job like this, you're thick. You
          know there's some nights I just can't stand it, I
          can't. I want to stand up on top of the bar and shout:
          I've got 'O' levels, I've got 'A' levels and a
          Bachelor of Arts Degree. So don't condescend to
          me, don't pretend you feel sorry for me and don't
          treat me like I can't read or talk or join in any of
          your conversations because I can. I see these
          teenage-like men and women with their well-cut
          suits and metal briefcases, discussing the City and
          the arts and time-shares in Tuscany, and I'm

jealous, because I can't work out how they've
achieved that success. It's so difficult. You see I
want to be a photographer, take portraits. I won a
competition in a magazine. It was this photo of a
punk sat in a field on an old discarded toilet. It was
brilliant. Anyway, after college I had this wonderful
idea that I'd go to London with my portfolio. I was
confident that I'd get loads of work. But it wasn't
like that. The pictures were great they said, but
sorry, no vacancies. My mum said I was being too
idealistic wanting it all straight away. My dad said I
should settle for a job with the local newspaper,
snapping Miss Gazette opening a shoe shop. No
thanks. Now he thinks I'm wasting my degree. I was
the first in the family to get one so it's not gone
down very well. My head's in the clouds he said,
life's not that easy. But it is for some people, like I
said, I see them in here. So why should I be
different, have they tried harder or something?
Maybe they're lucky or it's because they speak nice.
It's so frustrating because I know how good I am.
My dad's right, you know, in some ways: I'm stuck
here, wasting away. I do it for the money, that's all.
But it won't be forever, no chance. I'm applying for
assisting jobs, and as soon as I get one, don't worry.
I'm off. I'm now on plan two: Start at the bottom
and work up. It might take me years, I know that,
but it's what keeps me going between the lager and
the leftovers. The fact that I know I'll make it in the
end.

(*The action starts once more.* CAROL *is rather on the
outside.* MEL *and* NICKY *feature,* ADELE *serves
elsewhere.*)

MEL   She's funny about that isn't she?

NICKY   Who?

MEL   Carol.

NICKY   Funny about what?

MEL   People thinking she's thick.

NICKY   Well she's only young.

MEL   Yeh, she's a bit of a snob, I mean I don't give a toss what they think about me, but she's always making a point of it. Like she's more special.

NICKY   Well some of us have got ambitions, you know Mel, some of us aren't satisfied with just being here.

MEL   There's nothing wrong with working here. We can't all be brain surgeons Nicky.

NICKY   I know that.

MEL   Oh the way you were talking I thought you were going to tell me, you were running off to be Chiropodist to the Queen.

NICKY   Not quite.

CAROL   (*coming to* MEL *and* NICKY) Have you seen Mario? He looks like Pavarotti . . . he's strutting about like a prima donna.

NICKY   Why? Is he on the war path?

CAROL   He's got this idea.

MEL   What? Is it about the short measures?

CAROL   I don't believe that man sometimes . . .

MEL   What what tell us what . . . ?

NICKY   Look out, he's watching.

CAROL   Smile . . .

ALL   Hiya!

(*They serve and move away. Contemporary disco music plays. We are in a typical young women's clothing store. The supermarket girls are buying their outfits for the big night.* MEL *has become the shop assistant.*)

ALL	Top Shop!
ADELE	Sharon . . . can't spend a lot . . .
CAROL	Got a credit card.
NICKY	Elaine . . . wanting something special.
MEL	Assistant . . . It's three garments and no more.
CAROL	Where's Susan?
ADELE/ NICKY	Gone to the market . . .
ALL	Uggh!!!!!
CAROL	Do you have to get really dressed up?
NICKY	It's a posh place, yes.
ADELE	And I'll tell you something, Andy King gets in there!
NICKY	Does he?
ADELE	Yeh I've seen him.
NICKY	Brilliant . . .
CAROL	Keep your hands off him you cheeky get, I want him.
NICKY	No chance, I'm the birthday girl!
MEL	How many have you got there love?
CAROL	A skirt and some jeans.
MEL	Take this shirt in with you love.
CAROL	Yes.
MEL	It's three garments.
CAROL	Thanks.
MEL	Just through there . . . three love?

NICKY   Yes.

MEL   In you go.

ADELE   I think I've got eleven, I can't decide what to go for.

MEL   Well you'll have to leave some here.

ADELE   Ok.

MEL   In you go.

CAROL/
ADELE/   Get her . . .
NICKY

CAROL   I hate these communal ones, everybody looks at you. (*Looking around.*) I don't like what she's got on.

ADELE   I've got one of them.

CAROL   Well it's not that bad, just doesn't suit her probably.

ADELE   No.

CAROL   Have you heard this music, chuffin' hell.

NICKY   Fine Young Cannibals, it's great.

CAROL   Not in here though, it feels like Roland Gift's watching you get changed.

ADELE   You should be so lucky. (*The girls mime undressing.* MEL [*The Assistant*] *watches.*)

CAROL   Mind you he'd probably be sick if he saw me get changed with my legs.

ADELE   There's nothing wrong with your legs.

CAROL   There is. They're massive.

NICKY   You're paranoid.

CAROL   They are though, look.

NICKY   Don't be daft.

CAROL   Mind you when you look at her over there I don't suppose mine are that bad.

ADELE   Where?

CAROL   In that corner.

ADELE   Oh I wouldn't dare.

NICKY   She's no idea.

ADELE   Trying a mini skirt on with a figure like that.

CAROL   She looks a right state, too thin, she's a stick insect.

NICKY   Look at that one, she's got no bra on.

ADELE   Dirty bitch, who does she think she is.

NICKY   Nice tits though.

ADELE   Yes.

CAROL   Makes my nipples sore that.

ADELE   What?

CAROL   Not wearing a bra . . .

NICKY   I wish I'd put some decent knickers on.

CAROL   I wish I'd shaved my legs . . .

NICKY   She's nice.

CAROL   Who?

NICKY   Oh yeah I can see her in the mirror, nice figure.

CAROL   Wish I looked like that, the cow.

ADELE   She's got a bit of a dog face though.

CAROL   Ugly.

NICKY	Yeah.

ADELE I think this is one of them things that look alright on the hanger.

NICKY/
CAROL Mmmmmm.

ADELE I'll swop it for something else.

CAROL She's fat, look at her she's fat, she's very fat.

NICKY Enormous.

ADELE Yes she's fat, she's an elephant.

ALL Whew, thank God, someone's fatter than us.

CAROL It's like trying to pack your suitcase when you're going on holiday.

NICKY What?

ADELE Her trying to get into that. And look at them spots on her back.

NICKY Horrible.

CAROL I've got spots on my back.

NICKY But you're not wearing a backless dress.

CAROL We shouldn't say anything, it might be glandular.

ADELE Could be.

CAROL Oh I feel sorry for her don't you?

NICKY What's this dress look like?

ADELE Oh, it looks lovely that.

CAROL I wish I was as thin as you, you can wear anything.

NICKY Do you think it's too short?

ADELE No it's lovely.

CAROL   Flattering.

ADELE   Sexy.

NICKY   I quite like it.

CAROL   But it'll look better with stilettos instead of them
           trainers.

NICKY   I know that stupid. I think I like what she's trying
           on better.

CAROL   No, it looks cheap that, get that it suits you.

ADELE   I don't like any of these. (*To* MEL.) Excuse me,
           excuse me can I swop these for three other things?

MEL   Just come out and get them.

ADELE   I can't can I? I'm in my undies. (*To others.*) Silly
           cow.

MEL   Alright which do you want?

ADELE   That blue dress, no the dark one, that skirt and that
           little top. No, no that one, that's not mine.

MEL   This one?

ADELE   Yes. Thanks, thanks a lot.

           (NICKY *and* CAROL *have been trying on clothes.*
           CAROL *is struggling into a pair of jeans.*)

CAROL   I can't get these jeans on me.

ADELE   What size are they?

CAROL   A ten.

NICKY   They should fit.

CAROL   It's my legs, I've told you.

ADELE   They're probably small fitting.

CAROL   It's no good, I can't suck my legs in.

ADELE   Lie on the floor.

CAROL   They're meant for people with no legs.

ADELE   You what?

CAROL   This style. It's meant for people like you with no legs.

ADELE   Skinny legs you mean.

CAROL   You know what I mean.

NICKY   Lie down. They'll zip up then, that's what I do with mine.

CAROL   I'll feel stupid.

ADELE   Lie down.

NICKY   You can't wear jeans tonight anyway.

CAROL   I know, but they're for my holidays.

ADELE   Bloody hell, miss money bags. Elaine?

NICKY   Alright here we go . . .

ADELE   Breathe in!

CAROL   I am, you cheeky cow . . .

NICKY   It's no good, it's useless. (MEL *is staring at them.*)

CAROL   What's she looking at?

NICKY   Take no notice.

CAROL   She thinks she's something special just because she works in here.

ADELE   Shut up will you and try a bigger size.

CAROL   Are you having that dress Elaine?

NICKY   I think so.

ADELE   I'm going to get this lycra thing to go with my
         jacket.

NICKY   Nice. I need some earrings as well.

CAROL   Will you wait until I try some more jeans on?

ADELE   Well hurry up!

CAROL   (*leaning out to the assistant with her coat hanger*)
         Excuse me, could you swop me these for a size
         twelve?

MEL   I'm sorry but we've no twelves left in that size.

CAROL   Have you got any large fitting tens?

MEL   All our tens are small fitting.

CAROL   Are you sure?

MEL   Absolutely.

CAROL   What about a small fitting fourteen?

MEL   We're all out of fourteens, they've been ever so
         popular. There should be some more in next week
         sometime.

CAROL   I might call back then.

MEL   Sorry.

ADELE   Come on, let's go to C & A.

         (*Music. Back to Shakers.*)

NICKY   Pizza pepperoni?

MEL   One calzone.

ADELE   Seafood pasta.

CAROL   I'm coming through watch your backs please.

NICKY   Pizza, Four Seasons.

MEL   Pizza Mexicana?

ADELE   Does anyone want this seafood pasta?

NICKY   Pizza Americano?

MEL   Mixed salad.

ADELE   Seafood bleeding pasta anybody?

CAROL   I'm coming through, one Spag Bol, with chips.

NICKY   Very continental.

ADELE   Listen, listen stop everything. Somebody in here has
           ordered seafood pasta, now will you please, tell me
           who it is?

CAROL   (*as a man*) Excuse me!

ADELE   Is it me or is this place getting worse?

CAROL   Have you heard about the shorts?

ADELE   Yeh, but less in the cocktails, what a lousy trick,
           they're watered down as it is.

CAROL   No, shorts to wear?

MEL   What?

CAROL   He's got this idea about us wearing shorts.

MEL   He's bloody had it, I'm not. What's he want me to
           wear shorts for? Last week the cheeky bastard said
           I'd got to lose some weight. I said to him, "you lose
           some weight you're nearly as wide as you are tall."

ADELE   Why shorts?

CAROL   To help boost custom.

MEL   I said to him, "hang on I like being this size, Mae
           West was this size, and nobody complained about
           her."

NICKY   Mae West wasn't that big.

MEL   You what?

NICKY   Nothing.

MEL   What did you say?

NICKY   Nothing.

MEL   Mae West was big.

ADELE   So when do we have to put 'em on?

CAROL   When . . . never.

ADELE   Typical.

CAROL   What is?

ADELE   It's what you expect isn't it, working in a place like this?

CAROL   Is it?

MEL   Mind your backs please.

NICKY   Coming through.

CAROL   Is it what you expect?

ADELE   Table four, oh the fat man's been sick.

ALL   Oh God . . .

NICKY   Where's the mop?

ADELE   It's all over the floor.

NICKY   Oh my it stinks awful.

MEL   What is it?

ADELE   I think it's seafood pasta.

           (*Music. Supermarket girls are getting ready for the
           night ahead.* NICKY *is ironing,* CAROL *is under a*

sunlamp, ADELE *sits in a face mask. They are frozen in position until the music finishes.*)

ALL   "Getting ready for the party."

ADELE   Sharon, white-faced.

CAROL   Tracey, red-faced and dreaming of sun-kissed beaches.

NICKY   Elaine, dreaming of balloons, party poppers and passionate possibilities.

MEL   Susan, loaded down and late.

ALL   As usual!

MEL   Hi ya everybody, I'm here! Chuffin' busses they're never on time. They make me sick. I've bought my heated bendy rollers and my tongs and my diffuser so my hair doesn't go frizzy. I've got some gel and wax and thickening lotion but I couldn't find my mousse so you'll have to lend me some.

NICKY   You won't be able to hold your head up if you put all that stuff on. Hi ya Susan.

MEL   Hi. (*To audience.*) She gets right up my arse, her.

NICKY   (*to audience*) She gets right on my tits.

MEL   Anyway, I've got some of them More cigarettes as well, long and brown I think they look great.

NICKY   Don't smoke them near me, I can't stand it, it'll make my dress stink.

MEL   Don't worry I won't. What's up with Shaz? Aren't you talking or what?

ADELE   (*through an almost closed mouth as if wearing a face mask*) I can't.

MEL   You what?

NICKY   She can't.

MEL   Uggh! What's that stuff on your face?

ADELE   Face mask.

MEL   (*picking up an imaginary bottle and reading*)
             "Avocado and cucumber, the first step to a more
             beautiful you." I'll tell you something, it's
             definitely working. You look a lot better with that
             on than you ever did before.

ADELE   Don't make me laugh.

NICKY   Don't make her laugh.

MEL   Aggh, don't move it's cracking.

ADELE   Go away, go away will you!

MEL   Too late, it's gone.

ADELE   Shit.

MEL   You'll be alright . . .

ADELE   Well I have had it on ages. (*She mimes removing the
             face mask and makes appropriate noises.*)

NICKY   I've finished with the ironing board Shaz.

CAROL   (*coming out of freeze*) What am I gonna do? Look at
             my face!

NICKY   It's bright red.

CAROL   I know that.

MEL   What's happened?

ADELE   She's been on the sunbed.

ALL   Oooo . . . errr.

CAROL   I've only had fifty minutes.

ADELE   You're not used to it.

MEL · It's because you've got fair skin.

CAROL I can't go out like this.

NICKY Powder it down.

CAROL I can try.

ADELE I'm going to have a bath. (*She uses the bar as a bath.*)

MEL Shit. There's a ladder in my tights.

CAROL I've got to shave my armpits yet.

MEL And I only bought them today.

NICKY I've got some spare ones in my bag.

MEL They won't fit me.

ADELE They will, they fit any size. (*Grimace to audience from girls.*)

CAROL Have you got any hair removing cream?

ADELE In the bathroom!

CAROL Thanks.

NICKY I'll have to cover up my spot.

CAROL I'll have to cover up my face.

MEL Can I borrow some perfume, I love that Giorgio.

ADELE Plug in them rollers, I'll need them in a minute.

NICKY They won't work if your hair's wet.

ADELE I'm going to dry it first.

CAROL Will you put my nail vanish on for me, I can't do it with my left hand.

NICKY No, go away you stink of hair remover.

CAROL   (*as if it's on her legs and under her armpits*) I've
          got to give it ten minutes.

NICKY   Phewgh, you're like a dog that's been out in the
          rain. Can I borrow your mascara?

MEL   Yes . . . Do I look fat in this dress?

ALL   (*unconvincingly*) No . . .

ADELE   You look alright.

MEL   But does my bum look massive?

ADELE   Your hair looks really nice.

CAROL   I look like a tomato and smell like an old dish-
          cloth.

NICKY   Do you think Andy King will turn up?

ALL   God, Andy King!

MEL   Why?

NICKY   Just wondered.

CAROL   Oh yes?

NICKY   Our Sandra said he told her he thought I was alright.

ADELE   He never!

NICKY   He did.

CAROL   He's gorgeous, he can put his slippers under my bed
          any time.

MEL   Tracey! God!

ADELE   Well you've got no chance 'cos it sounds like it's
          Elaine he's after.

CAROL   Well that's bloody typical that is. Listen can you
          see my blackheads?

NICKY   I hope he will be there, you never know what might happen.

ADELE   Can you see my double chin?

MEL   Can you smell my hair spray?

CAROL   Can you smell my bad breath?

NICKY   Can you see my VPL?

ALL   Oh we'll never be ready!

(*Music. Back at the bar.*)

NICKY   Have you seen what some of these girls are wearing? Fashion victims.

CAROL   Thank you Selina Scott.

ADELE   Is it okay, but I'll have to go early?

MEL   You what?

ADELE   I'll have to go early.

MEL   What for?

ADELE   Get the last bus.

MEL   What's up with taxis?

ADELE   Are you going to pay for one?

MEL   No.

ADELE   Well I'll have to go half an hour early then.

MEL   Oh right, I'll go early as well then.

ADELE   Don't be childish.

MEL   I want to get home and see Steve, I don't want to be here, I can think of better things to do.

ADELE   It's only this once.

MEL   I've heard that before.

CAROL   What's your problem Mel? You're getting engaged, you're doing what you want.

MEL   Well look this is a job, we get paid to work so many hours, let's work them. I'll tell you what Adele. Why don't you just come in on Thursdays?

NICKY   What, every Thursday?

ADELE   I'm not talking to you, you're not worth it Melanie.

NICKY   Oh Melanie . . . ?

CAROL   I'll cover Adele's tables.

MEL   That's not the point is it? We're always covering for you in some way, I'm pig sick of covering for her.

ADELE   Alright you go early all next week, I'll make arrangements, I'll cover for you.

CAROL   What is the point Mel, I don't get it?

MEL   The point is, she should either have a job or be a mother.

ADELE   Millions do both.

MEL   Do they?

ADELE   They have to.

MEL   You can't do both it's obvious.

ADELE   And you know do you?

MEL   I know we're carrying you.

ADELE   How am I supposed to live? I don't even get maintenance payments.

MEL   And you're never here on time. What is it between you and Mario eh? It can't be doing a three year old much good being dragged around to God knows

where every night. Then being collected by her
mother in the morning.

ADELE   That's why I want to go early.

MEL   I mean the poor kid won't know where she is.

ADELE   Don't you bring Emma into this, because you don't
         know shit from butter.

MEL   Don't I?

NICKY   Never eat her sandwiches Adele.

MEL   You think you know everything don't you?

NICKY   Hey come on you two, leave it. There's a lot to do
         without all this.

ADELE   Shut up Nicky.

NICKY   Don't start on me.

ADELE   Just keep your beak out.

NICKY   Oh I like how it's all suddenly my fault.

ADELE   Just shut up.

NICKY   Sorry I spoke.

CAROL   Let's forget it, people are looking.

ADELE   Let them.

CAROL   Adele? Don't . . .

ADELE   Let 'em, let 'em look. I'm not bothered. Let the
         whole lot of 'em look, I couldn't give a toss.

MEL   She'll end up like her mother, if you ask me.

CAROL   Let it drop now.

MEL   And let's face it, her mother doesn't know where
         she is . . .

NICKY   Leave it Melanie . . .

MEL   Doesn't know what she wants.

ADELE   Why? Do you?

CAROL   Hey come on leave it alone, everybody's looking over here.

MEL   I know what I want . . .

ADELE   Do you?

MEL   Yeh I do. And I wouldn't treat a kid of mine like that.

ADELE   Wouldn't you?

NICKY   Let's just get on with the job shall we?

MEL   No I wouldn't . . . I mean look at yourself Adele, your life's an accident just waiting to happen.

ADELE   Let me tell you something, my little girl wants for nothing, she's happy, and she loves me and I love her more than you'll ever love anybody. Because you're too bitter and twisted to love anybody except yourself.

MEL   Piss off!

ADELE   I hope Steve realizes what he's letting himself in for.

MEL   Well he won't run off with somebody else, I'll tell you that much.

ADELE   And you're sure of that are you?

MEL   Yeh I am.

ADELE   Yeh I thought that I was sure. I thought it was going to be all hearts and flowers. Me and Craig were the perfect couple. Holding hands and kissing in public. Loves sweet dream . . . then Emma came along.

CAROL   Leave it Adele.

MEL   Well you know what you could have done.

ADELE   He wanted me to, she was an accident, anyway obviously I didn't. Debts built up. we started to argue, he started staying out, sounds like the routine thing but when it happens to you you can't believe it.

NICKY   Did you know her?

ADELE   I'd seen her. What hurt the most was that he told me he was looking for work. But he wasn't he was looking for her, and then he'd come home and I'd cook him his teas. So when you're cooking Steve's tea don't ask him where he's been, because if he's lying, it'll tear you up inside.

MEL   Yeh thanks I'll bear that in mind.

ADELE   I want to get out, I do, I want to get out of this rut, break away. I can't stand the facade, the show, the smiling, the grinning, the sniggers behind your back, the comments, the insulting tips, the pretence that what we're offering is a touch of class. I need something more than this, I need something that I can grab a hold of, something that I can call mine. I don't need a man, don't get me wrong, I thought I did, I don't, what I want is another chance. A chance to start over . . . And you know I probably would wear the shorts if he asks us, I'd probably go topless, get my tits out, wear tassels on the ends, and paint them the colours of the rainbow. I'd probably do whatever it needs to stay here, because at the moment, I've got no choice. I can't see anything that's going to make things better for me. Right now wearing a pair of shorts in a bar is just a matter of acceptance, because there's nothing else. It's just a teardrop in an ocean of worries.

Pause

ALL   Can we have some service.

ADELE   Coming . . .

(*The birthday girls enter Shakers all excited. They have already had a few drinks.*)

CAROL What about this? ZZZZZZZZ.

ADELE You daft cow, look at me, I'm covered in silly string!

MEL You look like a shopping basket.

NICKY We've got a table booked.

CAROL It's her birthday!

MEL Isn't it fantastic!

NICKY I think we're sitting over there.

ADELE I love the colours.

MEL I love the tables.

CAROL I love it all, it's gorgeous.

NICKY Is Andy King here?

CARLO Can't see him. Ooo, that wine's made me giggly has it you? (*All giggle.*)

ADELE We're going to have a great time.

MEL We're going to have a laugh.

NICKY Is Andy King here?

ADELE I'm having a prawn cocktail, garlic bread, spaghetti bolognese, a side salad, chocolate ice cream and a coffee.

CAROL Listen to her, you've not even looked at the menu.

ADELE It's what I always have.

NICKY Shall we have a drink first?

MEL Another!

ALL   Yeah!

CAROL   Let's all have a *Bloody Mary*.

ADELE   Bloody hell!

NICKY   Four *Bloody Marys*!

MEL   I love birthdays!

CAROL   I do.

MEL   Bloody hell it's strong.

CAROL   What is?

MEL   *Bloody Mary*.

ADELE   Oh I love it in here, it's fantastic.

NICKY   Oh my God.

ADELE   It's so classy.

MEL   I know it's brilliant.

NICKY   Oh God . . . look . . .

CAROL   What?

NICKY   Look there.

ADELE   Where?

NICKY   There, there, don't all look at once.

MEL   Where?

NICKY   Oh God. Look who it is.

CAROL   Which one?

MEL   Who do you mean, pizza face?

ADELE   Ughhh.

NICKY   No no . . . oh I can't move . . . look.

MEL   Where where . . .

ADELE   Who is it?

CAROL   What's she on about?

NICKY   Oh God I just can't believe it . . . it's him!

ALL   Who? (*A beat.*)

NICKY   Andy King!

            (*Music. The four girls react as if they have seen
            Andy King, and they blow kisses and wave to him
            and the lights fade to black.*)

            End of Act One

ACT TWO

*The set as before. House lights, music. The four actresses are
on stage, in a freeze. Lights, and with energy they come
downstage as the "boys".*

CAROL   And in we come, straight out of the car, straight
into the bar.

ADELE   The boys is what we are.

MEL   Dressed in our designer gear.

NICKY   Looking like men who drink Belgian beer.

MEL   We are talced and fresh, wearing splash-on *Polo*,
and minty foot deodorant.

CAROL   And teeth gleaming white, like George Michael.

NICKY   It's cold outside but we don't care, a flimsy top is
all we wear.

ADELE   We arrive at the door, our hair gel in place, and our
car keys dangling from our fingertips.

NICKY   Hi.

CAROL   Hi.

MEL   Hi.

CAROL   We assume that everyone in the bar is watching our
every step.

MEL   Our every move.

CAROL   (*hands through hair*) I am gorgeous.

ADELE   So am I.

NICKY   I love myself.

CAROL   We cooly adjust ourselves. (*They adjust their
crotch.*) And laugh nervously. (*All nervous laugh.*)

NICKY   We look cool but sexy. Like a cross between Tom
           Cruise and River Phoenix.

ADELE   A sort of river cruise.

MEL   And the gum? (*They all mime the gum.*)

NICKY   In goes the gum.

ALL   Thud. (*As the gum enters their mouth.*) Chew. (*They
           chew the gum.*)

ADELE   And another casual look around the place, eye out
           for the skirt.

MEL   If it moves take it to bed, if not stick it on your
           windscreen. Mark and Bernice, Radio One FM, the
           business.

NICKY   Trev and Val Radio One road show.

CAROL   Sound your horn if you had sex last night.

ALL   (*horn*) Road hog.

NICKY   And surfers do it stood up. (*Laugh.*)

CAROL   Rugby players do it in the scrum. (*Laugh.*)

MEL   Sky divers do it head first. (*Laugh.*)

ADELE   Hairdressers do it from behind.

ALL   Wooooooooohhh.

ADELE   And then I spot one. Oh yes, behind a plastic palm,
           sat near Andy King.

MEL   Andy King? Is he in?

CAROL   Over there?

NICKY   A God amongst men.

MEL   Who is he with . . . ?

CAROL   He looks fantastic.

ALL   Yeh.

ADELE   Oh look, the bird sat near Andy King, she's walking
             to the cig machine. Big tits, no tights, arse like a
             peach, I like to bite into that.

CAROL   Where is she?

ADELE   Passing one of the waitresses.

CAROL   Oh yeh.

ADELE   Over my left shoulder, two o'clock to the bar, five
             o'clock to the ciggy machine. (MEL *has become the
             girl.*)

CAROL   Nice one.

ADELE   So over to the ciggy machine I glide. (ADELE *crosses
             to* MEL *who is at a cigarette machine.*)

MEL   Shit.

ADELE   Isn't it working?

MEL   No. (*To audience.*) He thinks that I'm a bimbo but
             I'm really intelligent.

ADELE   Let me have a quick look. Huhu. A masculine boot
             should sort this out. I do Thai Kick Boxing you see.
             There, boot. (*Mimes a boot.*) There we are. Look
             'doll', twenty John Player Specials.

MEL   Thanks.

ADELE   No problem. My name's Matt.

MEL   Thanks Matt, but I wanted Benson & Hedges, bye.

ADELE   She walks off, shit, lost my cool.

NICKY   What happened?

ADELE   Oh man.

MEL   (*now one of the boys again*) Go on what happened!

ADELE   What a dog, breath like camel shit.

MEL   She looks fantastic.

ADELE   Yeh but up close, really rough, I think, she's
          married, she's deaf, she's blind she's fat, she's
          broke my cool, let's laugh it off.

CAROL   What happened, what went wrong?

ADELE   I just can't understand it.

MEL   Did you tell her your wear Ted Baker shirts?

ADELE   I said I know the Blow Monkeys, watch MTV and
          shop at Paul Smith.

MEL   Did you shave?

ADELE   With *Ronson*.

NICKY   What about teeth?

ADELE   *Plax* mouth wash.

NICKY   Arm pits.

ADELE   *Armani* roll on.

MEL   Maybe she thought you were dull?

ADELE   Give us a break.

NICKY   Maybe she thought you were gay?

ADELE   Come on?

CAROL   Maybe she just wasn't interested . . .

ALL   Don't talk crap!

ADELE   Let's have another round of Malibu and piss off down to *Browns*. Yeh.

ALL   Yeh.

ADELE   Great stuff.

ALL   Hey you. I'll have a Marra Bubu.

CAROL   What's a Marra Bubu?

ALL   Nothing Yogi.

NICKY   Let's get some more drinks.

ALL   Yeh.

CAROL   Hey you, can we have some service?

MEL   Come on love.

ADELE   Can we have some service down the cool end of the bar darlin'?

MEL   Hey you with the tits, what you doing later? Well do it on your own you ugly cow!

ADELE   She really is ugly. Hey call the ugly police.

CAROL   Can we have some service?

ADELE   Hey you. At last. What do we want?

NICKY   I'll have a *Malibu*.

MEL   And me.

CAROL   And me.

ALL   Right, another round of *Malibus*.

        (*The boys dissolve to waitresses.*)

MEL   Another round of farts.

ADELE   Posey bastards.

CAROL   I bet they're loaded that lot, got their money from Daddy's business. I've seen tramps with more manners.

NICKY   They're just having a night out, having a laugh.

MEL   At whose expense?

ADELE   You're lively at this hour aren't you?

MEL   I think she's on a promise.

CAROL   Yeh it's the bloke with the big ears and the glasses.

MEL   What, Pebble-dash Man?

NICKY   (*joking*) Chance would be a fine thing.

ADELE   Maybe it's the Wig Man but she daren't tell us?

NICKY   Like I said, I've had some good news today, that's all.

MEL   What?

NICKY   (*to* MEL) Look at you.

ADELE   Go on, what is it?

NICKY   Ah ha, interested are you?

CAROL   Anything to get out of here.

NICKY   Yeh well I've got a job.

MEL   Oh yeh what doing, dressing up in a bear's outfit and handing out leaflets?

NICKY   No, but it's something different.

MEL   So is dressing up as a bear.

NICKY   Dancing.

ADELE   Where?

NICKY   On a cruise.

MEL   A cruise.

CAROL   How long have you been dancing?

NICKY   I've done it for years, from being a kid.

ADELE   When do you start?

NICKY   In a month.

(*The others are green with envy.*)

CAROL   A month, that's good that's great, well done. That's great. A cruise?

MEL   My sister went on a cruise. It's a bit boring . . . She didn't like it.

ADELE   You'll see the world.

CAROL   I think it's great.

ADELE   Where do you go first?

CAROL   Bahamas would be nice.

ADELE   Or Florida.

NICKY   Norway.

MEL   Eh? You'll freeze to death.

CAROL   Norway.

MEL   What's in Norway?

CAROL   Fjords. Snow. Saunas.

ADELE   Norway?

CAROL   Pine furniture.

NICKY   Think of me in a month's time, the lights, the roar
         of the greasepaint, the smell of the crowd. I've
         always wanted to do it and at last I'm giving it a go.

MEL   I don't fancy that, living out of a suitcase. I
         wouldn't like it, I like my home comforts too much.

CAROL   Cross country skiing . . .

MEL   I'm happy being normal.

NICKY   You're normal?

CAROL   You'll send us a postcard won't you Nicky?

NICKY   Course I will.

ADELE   A cruise you lucky sod.

MEL   Yeh but Norway?

CAROL   Could be worse.

MEL   Could it?

         (*The lights fade. A spotlight outlines* NICKY. *The
         others freeze.*)

NICKY   I know they're jealous of me. I don't blame them,
         no one wants to stay here. It's funny though now I
         can escape, I'm bloody scared to death. Nine
         months, it's a long time, what if I don't make any
         friends? What if I get seasick, or food poisoning, or
         get lost somewhere in a forest and have to live with
         a tribe of eskimos and never come home again? I
         know I'm being stupid. My mind's gone haywire.
         But deep down I'm a panicker, I can't help it, but I
         am. And I know it's what I wanted, but in reality
         it's frightening leaving it all . . . your mum, your
         dad, your mates. I'm excited as well though, don't
         get me wrong. I wouldn't forego the opportunity,
         it's a chance in a lifetime: travel, freedom,
         celebrity. Oh yeh, I've definitely got to go! But the
         actual job? I wouldn't tell the others but more than

anything I'm apprehensive about that. I've got to
lose some weight for a start, some of the costumes
are ever so small, sequins and all that stuff, but
there is some topless as well. It's classy, it's all part
of the dancing. But it's getting over that first time
isn't it? Then I'm sure I'll be alright. You see to be
honest it took me about four days to get them out
when we went to Ibiza and then I laid on my front. I
suppose though they're alright, even though I'm not
Bridget Nielson. And they did look at them so if
they were awful they wouldn't have had me. Like I
said I'm sure I'll get used to it. It's all the
excitement, it makes you nervous I don't know
black from white. But I'm sure it will be brilliant,
I'm sure it will. I mean the world will be my oyster,
I can't believe it! That's the thing though isn't it?
What do you do when a dream comes true? What do
you dream of then?

(CAROL *and* MEL *are seated at two chairs. They are
Mr and Mrs Trendy.* NICKY *watches as* ADELE *takes
the order.*)

ADELE   One tired waitress.

NICKY   One *Tom Collins*.

CAROL   One trendy couple. In deep fried love.

MEL   Oh look at the menu. It's shaped like a cocktail
            shaker, isn't that clever. It's been designed that
            way.

CAROL   (*trendy man*) Yes that's why it's called *Shakers*.

            (*They laugh.*)

MEL   That's right. What do you fancy darling?

CAROL   What I fancy isn't on the menu.

MEL   Oh you're awful.

CAROL   I know.

ADELE   Excuse me, are we ready to order?

CAROL   (*abrupt*) We haven't had time to look at the menu yet.

ADELE   Sorry sir. I'll pop back in a moment. (*Aside.*) Twat.

MEL   I'd like to lick you all over.

CAROL   I don't know where to start (*The menu.*)

MEL   Did you hear me?

CAROL   You're wicked.

ADELE   I think I've pulled a bad straw.

NICKY   They look like a nice couple.

ADELE   Nice. Very nice. Jesus, these shoes.

MEL   Excuse me. (*Attracting attention.*) Excuse me . . . oi oi.

CAROL   Hello, Hello.

NICKY   I think they want to order.

CAROL   Hello

ADELE   I'm on my way. (ADELE *crosses.*) Ready to order, sir?

CAROL   Yes we'd like to start with garlic sweetcorn.

ADELE   Of course.

MEL   Oh no, I want the paté, I must have the paté.

CAROL   Do you have any paté?

ADELE   Sir?

MEL   What sort of paté do you have?

ADELE   What sort do you want you silly looking gett!

MEL	I'm awfully sorry?
ADELE	Madam, duck paté, liver paté.
MEL	I'll have the duck paté.
CAROL	One garlic sweetcorn, one duck paté, I'll take the lasagna, and Clarissa?
MEL	Could I, um. Have the . . .
ADELE	Come on pig breath.
MEL	Oh erm. Steak au poivre . . . no no.
ADELE	Hurry up.
MEL	Is the beef British?
ADELE	Madam.
MEL	Oh right, I'll try the . . . on no, I'll have the . . . erm, pasta, no no . . . I'll take the . . .
ADELE	For fuck's sake!
MEL	I'll have the fillet.
ADELE	Certainly madam. French fries, pomme frites? Side salad, baked potato?
MEL	Sorry.
ADELE	Are you flaming deaf, chips, lettuce or jacket spud?
MEL	I'll take the green salad, must watch the figure.
ADELE	Certainly. Wine?
MEL	Oh wine, wine.
CAROL	Wine?
MEL	Oh yes darling, wine, wine.

CAROL   Do you have any wine?

ADELE   It's on the back of the bloody menu.

CAROL   (*turns over menu*) Ah, ah here it is. Been there all the time. I think we'll take the Chateauneuf du Pape.

ADELE   Certainly. Would you like two straws?

CAROL   Sorry.

ADELE   I'll bring it straight away sir.

NICKY   And yet on the other hand there is always the couple who are not *au courant*.

         (MEL *and* CAROL *become Mr and Mrs Very Untrendy*.)

MEL   Menu's good in't it?

CAROL   What's it supposed to be?

MEL   Pepper pot isn't it?

CAROL   I thought it was a flask. What do you fancy?

MEL   Don't know.

CAROL   I fancy a lot of something, I'm starved.

ADELE   Excuse me sir, ready to order?

CAROL   No.

ADELE   Oh right, I'll be over by the bar, if you need me.

CAROL   I'll give you a shout.

MEL   I don't know where to start.

CAROL   What's this 'Entrees'?

MEL   Dunno . . .

CAROL Oi, oi. (ADELE *goes to them.*)

ADELE Ready to order sir?

CAROL Yes. I want the garlic sweetcorn. And two pints of lager and a bottle of red plonk.

ADELE Of course.

CAROL And she'll have the payt . . .

ADELE Payt?

CAROL Yeh a big slice of liver payt.

MEL And I want more than three slices of toast.

ADELE See what I can do.

MEL And a lot of butter, not just one frozen notch.

ADELE Certainly.

CAROL And two lasag-nees.

ADELE Would you like some chips and red sauce sir?

NICKY One *Zombie Voodoo*. A *Harvey Wallbanger*. And one *Screwdriver* coming up.

ADELE One *Mary Stewart*. And a *Johnny from London*.

MEL (*as* MEL, *moving*) Things are very hot.

CAROL (*as* CAROL, *moving*) Getting pretty hectic.

ADELE Behind the bar and in the kitchen.

NICKY Palms are sweating, feet are itching.

ADELE Every order is taken with a smile.

ALL Cheers.

NICKY Every bad joke returned with panache.

ALL   Oh that's really funny. (*A beat.*) Yawn.

ADELE   Ten o'clock and the place is heaving.

NICKY   The only room is on the ceiling. One *Blue Bols,* one *Side Car.*

CAROL   *Banana Monster.*

     (*Through this last order* NICKY *and* CAROL *have become a couple. They are seated.* MEL *and* ADELE *make cocktails.*)

ADELE   Oh God I think I've got this wrong now.

MEL   You what?

ADELE   I messed this up. I've got a *Havana Zombie* mixed up with a *Salty Dog.*

MEL   Well what are you making, a *Dog Zombie?*

ADELE   It's supposed to be a *Gin Sling.*

MEL   Could be a *Salty Zombie.*

ADELE   Help me Mel. I've wasted loads of booze, I've got all the names mixed up in my head.

MEL   It's because your mind's not on the job.

ADELE   What am I going to do?

MEL   Who is it for?

ADELE   The posh couple.

NICKY   You Uuuuu . . .

ADELE   Oh God they've seen me.

MEL   Just give it to her, it's a nice colour.

ADELE   It doesn't look much like a *Gin Sling* though does it?

MEL   Say it's a special.

ADELE   A special what?

MEL   I don't know, you're supposed to be the expert.

         (ADELE *takes the cocktail to the waiting couple.*)

CAROL   At last.

ADELE   Yes sorry about the wait, here's your cocktail . . .

CAROL   I ordered a *Gin Sling*.

ADELE   I know.

CAROL   Fine, take that away.

ADELE   Well you see you are our hundredth customer tonight, and so you win the surprise cocktail.

CAROL   But we've only just arrived and the place is seething.

ADELE   Hundredth cocktail customer, I mean.

CAROL   Oh well.

NICKY   That's great, thank you.

ADELE   Yes so you win tonight's surprise cocktail.

NICKY   Wonderful.

CAROL   What's in it?

ADELE   That's the surprise.

CAROL   It's tastes yummy. What's it called?

ADELE   It's erm. (*She looks around for inspiration.*) Oh erm . . . *Emergency Exit.*

CAROL   Oh, potent is it?

ADELE   You bet.

NICKY   Do you know I'm sure they make up these
          ridiculous names on the spur of the moment. You
          couldn't make me the *Two Hind Legs of an African
          Elephant* could you?

          (*The couple laugh.*)

CAROL   Oh, Gerald.

ADELE   Don't be so smart, you silly looking bastard.

NICKY   Sorry?

ADELE   I'm sorry sir, I'm afraid I don't know that one.

NICKY   It was a joke.

          (NICKY *laughs. Suddenly the four waitresses
          remember something. They have forgotten to sing to
          the birthday party. They rush around the stage, find
          the area where the birthday party group are sat.*)

ALL   Oh no . . .

          (*They regroup. The four waitresses stand in a line
          and sing happy birthday to four imaginary girls who
          are seated in a semi-circle in front of them. This is
          a routine which the cocktail waitresses are familiar
          with, however, on this occasion, they have omitted
          to discover the name of the person whose birthday it
          is, all saying different names together. Finally, they
          take four stools and become the girls at the party.*)

ADELE   It's getting late . . .

MEL   The restaurant's full . . .

CAROL   But in their little space . . .

NICKY   The birthday girl is tipsy and glowing in her lace . . .

MEL   She's had three more *Bloody Marys*.

ADELE   . . . And so have Sharon . . .

MEL   Sue . . .

CAROL   And Trace . . .

(*All hiccup.*)

MEL   That dress is smashing, I love it, I do I love it. Where did you get it? French Connection?

CAROL   No, got it at George.

MEL   George?

CAROL   Yeh, George at Asda.

MEL   Oh it's lovely that.

CAROL   It's nice here innit?

NICKY   Haven't you been before?

ADELE   We used to come every Thursday after aerobics.

NICKY   We think we saw Jonathan Ross in here once, he was on location. He's ever so tall.

CAROL   I don't like him.

NICKY   I don't.

MEL   Does he play the piano with that group?

ADELE   No, that's Jools Holland. Jonathan Ross is the one with the suits.

MEL   Oh him, he's got a beard, does The Clothes Show.

CAROL   That's Jeff Banks. Somebody switch her off.

NICKY   It's packed out tonight.

ADELE   It's warm.

NICKY   I'm spinning.

CAROL   My face is on fire.

MEL   Don't worry you look alright.

NICKY   If you like tomatoes.

(*All laugh.* ADELE *becomes the waitress.*)

ADELE   And then: a flash, a scintilla! For Elaine a birthday treat. A crushed ice candy cocktail with a sparkler in it.

MEL   Mind your hair, it'll set on fire!

CAROL   Isn't it brilliant.

ADELE   Very, very neat.

ALL   Oh isn't it nice. Lovely. It's great!

NICKY   Oh no, everyone's looking.

ADELE   They're all glad it's not them.

NICKY   I'm embarrassed, God I'm embarrassed. Can you see Andy King?

CAROL   Can I hell, it's choc-a-bloc.

MEL   Isn't that him over there?

NICKY   Where? Oh yeh, he's looking at us, he can see me!

CAROL   I feel tiddly, I think it's this drink.

ADELE   (*who has now become* SHARON) He's waving.

NICKY   He's not! Can he see it's my birthday?

MEL   I think so, they're all waving. Come on wave at them. (MEL *begins to wave.*) Hey up. Ooooh.

NICKY   Don't!

CAROL   It's her birthday!

NICKY   Oh no!

ADELE   Twenty-one you cheeky sods.

MEL   I think he winked at you.

NICKY   Oh my heart's going, I've come over all queer.

CAROL   He's with somebody, she's just come back from the toilet!

MEL   Oh yes.

NICKY   Oh God.

ADELE   She's attractive.

NICKY   Oh well. I don't suppose he's that nice anyway . . .

CAROL   Hey watch this. A party popper!

           (*The miming of the party popper presents fun as we see it explode in the air.*)

ADELE   I've had a monster *Piña Colada*, I feel great!

MEL   I feel a bit sick, it's this wine. I'm not used to it.

NICKY   Do you think he's been going out with her long?

ADELE   Hey! Crackers . . .

ALL   Ohhh! Yehhhh! (*They mime the pulling of crackers, put on the hats, etc.*)

MEL   I've got a ring.

ALL   Urrerrmmm.

ADELE   I've got a hat. It's daft.

NICKY   It suits you.

CAROL   Hey listen to this. "The more you take the more you leave behind." What is it?

ADELE   Tablets?

MEL   Water?

NICKY   Girlfriends.

MEL   What?

CAROL   Steps, the more steps.

ALL   Oh yeah, good that.

CAROL   A toast to Elaine, twenty-one today.

ADELE   God bless you love.

            (*They all sing a verse of "Twenty-One Today."*)

NICKY   (*sings*) Happy birthday to you . . . (NICKY *is away,
            she improvises a tune, freezes upstage.* CAROL,
            ADELE *and* MEL *are downstage.*)

MEL   Nicky is unbelievable. She is always over the top. I
            mean who does she think she is, Bonnie Langford?

ADELE   She's happy that's all.

MEL   Do you really think she'll make it?

CAROL   Don't know. If she's determined.

MEL   I don't think she will.

ADELE   So that's the kiss of death for her . . . ?

CAROL   Why not?

MEL   I don't know. I think it's her nose. Her face,
            something. I wouldn't go on a cruise no way. It's
            something . . .

CAROL   Like what?

MEL   She's really too short for a dancer. That's why she's
          going on a cruise. If she was tall she'd be going to
          be a blue-bell girl. You see I know about these
          things. My cousin was an understudy on *Cats*, she
          was six foot two.

CAROL   Oh right.

MEL   In nine months time she'll be coming back here with
          her tail between her legs, asking Mario for work.

CAROL   I wouldn't argue about it. This place is going to
          close.

MEL   You what?

CAROL   It's going to change hands anyway.

MEL   You know what it'll be, a few new palms, a coat of
          paint, maybe some foreign beers, and it's more or
          less the same. We'll still be here. It's happening all
          over, it's like spring cleaning.

CAROL   So the punters think they're getting something new.

MEL   Maybe it'll become a MacDonald's.

CAROL   God forbid.

MEL   Well there isn't a MacDonald's around here for
          nearly two hundred yards.

CAROL   Do you know what is in a Big Mac?

ADELE   Don't please.

MEL   It could be like one of those trendy new places,
          there's one in Covent Garden. Thank God it's
          Sunday.

CAROL   Fridays.

MEL   You speak for yourself Carol.

ADELE   Oh we are on the ball tonight.

MEL   It'll be one of those places where the waitresses are
          employed because they are witty and smart.

CAROL   Unlike here, where they're shitty and fart . . . ?

ADELE   Does that include you?

MEL   You know the sort of place I'm on about, they wear
          odd socks and bumpers and wear hats with dog turds
          on them.

ADELE   Very witty.

CAROL   Very smart.

MEL   Joke turds. You can wear what you want, as long as
          it's stupid.

CAROL   Sounds like hell.

MEL   And they play Jazz music, and have trombones that
          come through the ceiling and pianos that play by
          themselves.

CAROL   It is hell.

MEL   Oh I think that'd be good. You could wear
          something different every day. I'd wear a badge on
          my bust with very small writing on it. It would say
          "If you can read this, you are two foot too close so
          knob off . . ."

ADELE   Well I wish you luck.

CAROL   Secretly, you really like it here don't you? Even
          though you complain all the time?

MEL   It's like this Carol, in the mad bad world as long as
          you do your job, you can complain as much as you
          want. No one can sack you for complaining, they
          can only get rid of you if you don't work.

CAROL   That sounds subversive.

MEL   Common sense if you ask me, take the money,
        complain as much as you want, and then run. Or in
        my case hobble.

ADELE   Sounds to me like you've got it all worked out.

MEL   Yeh it does doesn't it?

ADELE   Yeh.

MEL   Yeh that's me kid.

ADELE   Everything in it's place and a place for everything!

MEL   Yeh lucky old Mel.

ADELE   You'll probably be here when you're sixty.

MEL   If I'm lucky.

ADELE   Full of ambition aren't you?

MEL   Actually I am, yeh.

ADELE   Day in day out, no change. "Mel the constant." You
        should put that on a badge and all.

MEL   Yeh I might do.

ADELE   No troubles and no bloody worries . . .

        (*The lights slowly fade.* MEL *steps forward.*)

MEL   This job's not bad you know. I used to work in the
        supermarket, now that was mindless, sat about all
        day, bored out of your head, dreaming of the
        weekend. At least when you're here you can have
        the odd cig and a natter. You see I just want an easy
        life, no pressures. And I want someone to care for
        me, and I think I've found that with Steve, I do.
        Adele thinks she's the only one with problems? Oh
        God who is she kidding? Talk about skeletons in the
        cupboard, I've got a kitchen suite full of them. You
        see there's something I've got to tell Steve; I think
        it's only fair. You see when I was sixteen I used to

go to this tacky bar with my mates. I thought it was
neat. It had an awful painting of the Manhattan
skyline right around the walls. And a drawing of the
Statue of Liberty that was about nine times too big
sticking up from behind a skyscraper. The New
York Bar . . . oh what? . . . I thought it was great.
And I met this bloke there. Pete, he was a bar man.
He was a lot older than me and really good looking.
I thought he was great. We had a brilliant time, a
lot of laughs and I was still a virgin. He didn't force
me to sleep with him, but I fancied him that much
and it seemed the most exciting thing ever, that I
couldn't help myself. I wasn't stupid though. I tried
to get on the pill but I'd had jaundice when I was a
kid, so I ended up with a cap. I'm not kidding,
they're a right pain in the neck. I've got a coil now
so it's ok. Anyway we went on holiday for two
weeks to Scotland, I told my mum that I was going
with my mates. I thought I was pregnant when I
went but I didn't tell anyone. I was frightened, so I
put it to the back of my mind. But it was impossible
because I kept seeing pregnant women and mothers
with pushchairs and tiny clothes on hangers and
babies in magazines. So I went into the chemist and
searched amongst the Durex for a DIY testing kit.
Back in the camp site toilets I weed all over my
hands trying to get it in the test tube. Why do they
make them so small? Two hours later the change in
colour and the sickness in my stomach said
everything. I didn't really have time to think about
it. I asked for an abortion. I mean neither me or
Pete wanted to have this thing that would tie us
down forever . . . It's a big responsibility. And what
would my mum have said or my mates on the YTS?
And what about the rest of our lives? I was scared
as well, how could I look after a kid? I only had two
GCSE's I begged them to let me have it done up
there in Scotland, so no one would know. They put
me in this hospital by the sea. There were about
eight of us in the ward. All the others had fluffy
slippers and dressing gowns and orange juice by
their beds. I had to make do with a hospital nightie,
my stocking feet and a baggy combat jumper I'd
taken camping with me. It's soon done, you bleed a

lot and feel depressed, but it is a relief as well.
Sometimes I think about it, what it would be like
now. It upset me. I want to tell people, talk about it,
but I can't. The thing is should I tell Steve? We
want to get married and I know this time it's right.
He's got a good job, he's a roadie with a rock band,
we might even be able to buy a house. I want to tell
him because I want to be honest. But it can stop you
having kids altogether can't it? I'm frightened that
if he knows he'll leave me. No, I think I'll keep it a
secret between me and you. Don't tell anyone, will
you?

(*The lights fade slowly. Slow music. The evening is
creeping by. Lights fade at the end of* MEL's *speech.
A sudden rush of energy, as a theatre crowd returns
to Shakers for a post-show drink.*)

CAROL   Darling?

MEL   Darling?

CAROL   Darling's over here by the window.

ADELE   What a wonderful show.

NICKY   Wonderful.

MEL   I thought she was amazing.

CAROL   Wasn't she just.

ADELE   Breathtaking. I've seen all his work. Donald and I
        listen to the show on CD.

MEL   It really is the only way to listen.

CAROL   I wish I'd seen Elaine Page.

MEL   We saw her in London, she was ever so good. And
        do you know she's only quite tiny.

ADELE   Excuse me waitress, we're ready to order.

NICKY   It's based on a true story, apparently there was an
          Eva Peron.

CAROL   Really?

NICKY   Oh yes and she was Argentinian.

CAROL   Isn't that amazing?

ADELE   I thought it was a touch too long.

MEL   Yes I'd trim the second act.

ADELE   But I wouldn't cut the interval. Waitress?

MEL   Oh no I thought the interval was marvellous.

CAROL   Anyone for a drink?

ALL   I'll say. Yes. I think we all are.

MEL   Terry saw him at the health club.

ADELE   Who?

MEL   Che Guevara.

ALL   Really.

CAROL   Sidonie has bought a new horse, did I tell you?

ALL   Really?

MEL   Have you heard about the new, F-Plan diet.
          Apparently you can lose fifteen stone in a day.

ALL   Really?

NICKY   Well I was talking to one of the gals at the club and
          she said there was still a National Health service.

ALL   Really?

ADELE   Where?

NICKY   I think she said somewhere in Scotland.

MEL   Oh yes I think I've heard of Scotland.

ADELE   Don't you think it's marvellous now we all live in a
           classless society?

ALL   Oh yes.

MEL   Oh yes.

CAROL   Oh look at the chef.

           (*During this* MEL *has become the chef.*)

ADELE/   Oh isn't that good.
NICKY

CAROL   What's he doing?

NICKY   Tossing a pizza.

CAROL   Oh.

ADELE   We saw that done in Porto Banus.

ALL   Really?

ADELE   Yes the chef was Spanish.

NICKY/   How amazing.
CAROL

ADELE   They called him Carlos.

NICKY/   That's interesting.
CAROL

ALL   Waitress!!!

           (MEL *has entered with an imaginary pizza. The chef
           is Scottish.*)

MEL   Can you shout up when you make a bloody order, I
           can't hear you. Shout up. You're bloody useless.
           What you think I like making pizzas in public? You

must be bloody joking kiddo. This place is crap. I should have stayed on North Sea Ferries if you ask me. And the waitresses are bloody useless. (*Shouts.*) There's a steak burning here. Get your arse round here. I'll tell you what they bring the food back all the time, I've had seafood pasta coming back here all night. What I do is this, they bring it back, all coy and helpful, I slap it in the microwave pour some sauce over it and call it a brand new dish. If they bring a steak back complaining that it's not done, I turn it over slap two bits of parsley on it, three more chips, half a tomato and it's ready to go. (*Shouts.*) Steak Diane ready to go. God. I'll tell you this, when I'm feeling really vindictive I put things from my nose in the Pizza Margarita . . . spices it up bit. One Pizza Margarita ready to go!

(*A sudden burst of action.*)

CAROL   Irish coffee?

NICKY   Banana split?

MEL   Two brandies?

ADELE   Seafood pasta?

CAROL   Steak Diane?

MEL   Pizza Margarita madam . . . no no they're anchovies madam . . . yes I'm sure madam.

CAROL   What time is it?

NICKY   Ten to.

CAROL   Ten to what?

NICKY   Eleven.

CAROL   Last orders.

MEL   (*comes to them*) Mario says keep serving the bastards.

NICKY   Keep serving?

MEL   Yeh you know what that means.

NICKY   They'll stay and chat for two hours, then it's coffees
          and brandy till half one.

MEL   And we're to send a free bottle of bubbly to
          whoever's birthday it is.

CAROL   That man is so greasy.

NICKY   Hey who is that sat at table six?

MEL   Oh that's Andy King.

NICKY   Mmm very nice.

MEL   Oh no . . . too clean looking, I only like dangerous
          men.

NICKY   He is dangerous.

CAROL   What exactly does Steve look like, Mel? Freddy
          Krueger?

MEL   No more like Rutger Hauer actually, Carol.

NICKY   Oh yes, wet your knickers.

CAROL   Mmmm nice.

MEL   Who, Freddy Krueger?

CAROL   Andy King.

NICKY   Carol, you man eater.

CAROL   It's an aesthetic opinion Nicky, that's all. I bet he's
          very aggressive, probably breast fed.

MEL   Thank you Claire Raynor.

NICKY   Mmmm very nice.

CAROL   Nicky you're drooling.

NICKY   I know.

MEL   Yeh he's all right is Andy, he went to school with my cousin. She's 6'2".

NICKY   Do you know him?

MEL   I sort of know him to wink and nod at.

CAROL   So you don't know him?

MEL   No, not really.

ADELE   (*coming to them*) Have you seen Mario?

MEL   Yeh fat bloke, dodgy looking.

ADELE   I mean has he told you about these shorts?

NICKY   What?

ADELE   He's just told me he definitely wants us in shorts, from tomorrow, he wants to see how they look.

CAROL   That man is a pervert.

ADELE   He says we're to try 'em because they look more trendy.

CAROL   Trendy, it's so men can have a good look.

ADELE   I've seen 'em they don't look that bad.

CAROL   But it's the idea of it.

ADELE   They're quite smart actually.

CAROL   And where is it going to lead to? It'll be shorts first and then cami knickers, and then pink tutu's and then God knows what?

NICKY   Knee high Wellies?

CAROL   Maybe. And fat Mario will sell more champagne
        and whoever's working here then will be that cheap
        the punters'll think a fiver will get them a blow job.

MEL   I'd do it for twenty. I was joking. I wouldn't do it
        for a thousand.

NICKY   Dunno?

ADELE   Well we'll see what happens tomorrow then won't
        we. Because I've got a kid to feed Carol. I can't
        afford not to do what I'm told.

CAROL   So you'll wear 'em then?

ADELE   Yeh, and I might stick a flower up my arse and all.

CAROL   You're being selfish.

ADELE   No I'm not.

NICKY   I don't want anything to do with it, me.

ADELE   Well you're lucky aren't you?

NICKY   Yeh I am yeh, and I've worked bloody hard for it.

ADELE   Oh have you.

NICKY   Yes I bloody have.

MEL   Listen I'm wearing no shorts or nothing, but be
        honest Carol when we went out on Nicky's birthday
        you wore a dress that was that short, I could see
        your breakfast.

ADELE   Yeh you did.

NICKY   You've got nice legs.

CAROL   That was different.

MEL   Was it?

CAROL   I was wearing that for me.

MEL   So you're not bothered about men looking at your legs when you want them to?

CAROL   Going out for a meal is different isn't it. You're not on show. You're not seducing the punters' fantasies?

MEL   You what?

CAROL   I'll tell you this, if you wear them shorts tomorrow, I'll rip 'em off you.

NICKY   Oh you kinky bitch Carol.

ADELE   Oh yeh?

CAROL   Yes I mean it Adele.

ADELE   I'm sorry Carol, I am, honest. I don't want all this to happen, and I'm not thick. I know what you're on about.

CAROL   I do mean it. If you wear those shorts Adele, you're dropping us all in it. You just think about it . . .

ADELE   (*suddenly turning into another tone*) Can you finish your drinks off now please.

NICKY   Thank you ladies and gents, time to go home.

CAROL   Time please.

MEL   Twenty-one? Yeh happy birthday.

NICKY   I wonder if Vicky's burnt the meal? There's always somebody worse off than you are just think about that.

ADELE   I hope you freeze to death in Norway.

NICKY   You don't do you?

ADELE   No . . . no I don't . . .

MEL   Have you seen the toilets?

CAROL   What about 'em.

MEL   It's like the black hole of Calcutta; you can't move for hair spray.

(*Blackout. Lights up.* NICKY *still sniffing.*)

NICKY   So she says to me if you don't keep your bloody hands off him I'll slap you.

MEL   Did she? She must have seen us waving at him.

NICKY   As if I'm scared of her.

CAROL   She's a fart, you can tell from her handbag.

NICKY   I don't know what he sees in her.

ADELE   I don't.

NICKY   And I thought it was going to all work out tonight.

MEL   We've had a good time anyway haven't we?

NICKY   I suppose so.

ADELE   'Course we have. Who needs Andy King anyway?

NICKY   But I love him.

CAROL   You don't, you're drunk. She's drunk everybody just ignore her. God these mirrors really show up your spots.

NICKY   And I feel embarrassed.

ADELE   Hey look have I gone pale?

CAROL   I wish I had.

NICKY   I'll kill our Sandra for telling me lies.

MEL   Can I borrow your comb?

CAROL   Yes here. My hair's dropped.

ADELE   It suits you like that.

CAROL   What? A mess?

ADELE   No, that style.

CAROL   (*as if lifting up her skirt*) Here, have you seen this? I've got loads of cellulite.

MEL   I have.

ADELE   I can't see any.

CAROL   You can if you squeeze my bum.

ADELE   Oh yeh! Sago pudding!

CAROL   Is it that bad? That's it, I'm going to start doing my callanetics again.

NICKY   I've got cellulite, that's probably why he doesn't like me.

MEL   As if he can see it through your dress.

NICKY   I bet she's not got it, her he's with, she looks like a soddin' model.

CAROL   She looks like a tart. Have you got any hair spray?

ADELE   I have, there's just a bit left.

MEL   Do them callanetics work?

CAROL   Yes they're brilliant. You can lose a stone in half a day.

NICKY   Do you think she's nicer looking than me?

ADELE   Look, have a few more drinks and forget about it. It's your birthday, it's not every week that you're twenty-one!

NICKY   I just want to die.

MEL   It's them *Bloody Marys*, they're bloody lethal.

CAROL   I'm going to have another.

MEL   Well I've gone all dizzy.

ADELE   Don't be sick.

NICKY   You know something. I hate my face.

CAROL   Put a bag on your head!

NICKY   Ooooaah . . .

(*Music. We're no longer in the toilets.* CAROL, ADELE, NICKY *and* MEL *are reflecting on the last scene.*)

ADELE   There's another girl crying in the toilets.

NICKY   Oh well.

ADELE   Over a man.

CAROL   Pathetic.

NICKY   Who is it?

ADELE   Somebody, Andy King I think.

NICKY   Oh well.

MEL   Is she drunk?

ADELE   Looks like it.

CAROL   Ruled by their heads and not their hearts.

MEL   They're only having a good time.

CAROL   Are they?

ADELE   Yes they are.

CAROL   Well I suppose if that's all they've got to look forward to . . .

NICKY   What?

ADELE   Sometimes Carol you're depressing.

MEL   Yeh at least they're looking for a man Carol, and not just taking photos of them.

ALL   (*sarcastic reaction*) Oooooooohhhhhh.

(*The oooohhh becomes the Conga. They begin to Conga around the stage.*)

Na na na na na na - na,
We're getting very drunk now
We're getting very merry
Happy Birthday Elaine,
What a super party.

ADELE   I've got a silly hat on . . .

NICKY   I've ruined my mascara . . .

MEL   I've laddered all my stockings . . .

CAROL   I've stuffed my face quite stupid . . .

ALL   Na, na, na, na. Na, na, na na . . .

(*Gradually the noise fades as does the dance and the Conga is replaced with the four supermarket girls just outside Shakers Bar. NICKY [ELAINE] is still very tearful.*)

NICKY   I feel sick.

ADELE   You're right.

MEL   I feel fine now.

NICKY   Everything's spinning round.

CAROL   What time is it?

NICKY   Honestly, I think I'm going to faint.

CAROL   Go home then, 'cos I'll tell you sommat, you're getting on my nerves.

NICKY   I can't go home, it's my birthday.

ADELE   Why don't we go to a disco?

MEL   A club?

ADELE   Yeh.

CAROL   Brilliant. I could go on all night.

NICKY   Everything's ruined, nobody cares, nobody's
         bothered . . .

CAROL   Oh stop crying will you, it's been like being with
         Gazza for the last two hours.

NICKY   It's you, you don't know what it's like to be in love.

CAROL   In love? Isn't that supposed to make you happy?

ADELE   It can hurt though Trace.

NICKY   Yeh well it's hurting me now. I've got this awful
         pain in my chest.

CAROL   It's indigestion.

MEL   Or your bra's too tight.

ADELE   Too many anchovies early on.

NICKY   It's not. It's Andy King. He's my perfect man, I
         know it. It's just that he doesn't realize.

ADELE   Come off it, you've never even spoke.

NICKY   I have, I have . . .

MEL   When?

NICKY   At work, when I was on cereals, he came up and
         asked me where the Ready Brek was.

ADELE   Who wants a man who eats Ready Brek?

NICKY   I do . . . I do . . .

CAROL   Oh for God's sake.

MEL   It's alright Elaine love, come on, there'll be loads
          of nice blokes down the disco.

NICKY   I'm not bothered.

CAROL   Look, you've got to accept it, he doesn't like you,
          he's got a girlfriend and he doesn't like you!

MEL   Don't.

ADELE   I think men are overrated. I always have a better
          time on my own.

MEL   Is it starting to rain?

CAROL   Shit, come on let's leg it to *Pinocchio's*.

NICKY   I don't want to.

ADELE   Cheer up Elaine, you're only twenty-one once, you
          want to remember it as being happy.

NICKY   I can't.

CAROL   Oh leave her, she's a pain in the neck.

MEL   I'm getting wet through.

ADELE   Come on love.

NICKY   I don't want . . .

CAROL   Leave her . . .

MEL   We can't . . .

ADELE   She's pathetic . . .

CAROL   Leave her . . .

MEL   Oh alright . . . Thanks for the meal Elaine. My steak
          wasn't cooked, but it was lovely.

ADELE   Yes thanks, it was lovely.

CAROL   You'll be alright, get yourself a taxi.

NICKY   Aooh . . .

MEL   See you tomorrow.

ADELE   Is it far this disco?

CAROL   Not really.

ADELE   See you, take care . . .

NICKY   Aaaoooh . . .

MEL   Are you sure she's going to be alright?

CAROL   Look I don't care, she's driving me absolutely insane. I've heard there's a nice DJ at *Pinocchio's*.

MEL   There is . . .

CAROL   He's gorgeous, Bruno they call him.

ADELE   Brilliant! Let's get going then!

ALL THREE   Yehhh!

NICKY   (*shouting after them*) Hey! I've changed my mind, I think I might come with you! Hey! . . . Wait for me! . . . It's my birthday remember . . . Wait! . . . you bastards . . . Wait.

(*Lights. We are back in Shakers. The girls are bidding a number of clients "goodnight".*)

ADELE   Goodnight.

NICKY   Tara.

MEL   See you again.

CAROL   Drive carefully . . .

ADELE   Take care.

ALL   Goodnight!

NICKY   That's it then.

CAROL   Turn that bloody music off.

MEL   Yeh let's have a bit of peace and quiet.

NICKY   Oh I quite like it.

ADELE   I'm going to get off . . .

MEL   I think the air conditioning's come on.

CAROL   Oh great.

ADELE   I'll see you then shall I?

MEL   Look at the mess . . .

NICKY   Somebody's left their scarf.

ADELE   Is it okay?

NICKY   Just go Adele.

ADELE   Right . . .

CAROL   And think about tomorrow . . .

ADELE   I will.

NICKY   Go . . . or you'll miss the bus . . .

ADELE   Thanks.

CAROL   Go on . . .

ADELE   Hey you can have my tips.

NICKY   Brilliant.

CAROL   Look at her . . .

ADELE   See you then . . .

MEL   Adele get. Go on. Shoooo . . .

(*Silence.* ADELE *stops, turns to the audience. In spotlight.*)

ADELE You know at times like these I feel like they hate me for having Emma. I hate myself for having Emma. I hate Emma, I know, I shouldn't say things like that, but I have feelings inside that I don't know how to cope with because they're all mixed up with other feelings of love. You see right at this moment I've had enough, I don't want to get the bus, I don't want to walk up the estate. I don't want to pick up this sleeping thing and wheel her home, hopping she doesn't cry. I want just to be able to think about me, to watch the late night film on the telly and relax with a glass of wine. But I know that when I see her, her hair all floppy, I feel a love so strong, so like nothing else that it makes me glad to be alive. But I've got to stick at it until she starts school. Then it's got to change, for the sake of both of us. Do you know what I'd really like? To . . . work in a travel agents, sending lots of people to the sun. I'd get home early and Emma will run in from school and we'll laugh and look at her paintings. Maybe then I'll see my life in colour instead of black and white.

(ADELE *exits. Silence. Lights back to the bar.*)

MEL I think I might go early tomorrow.

CAROL Fine.

MEL About half eight okay?

NICKY Yeh, I'll go early Monday.

CAROL That music is ringing in my head.

NICKY Turn it back on . . .

CAROL Some nights I can't get to sleep because of the songs going round and round. I wake up the next day and I'm suddenly singing the lyrics to "I want to sex you up."

MEL   Look at the mess in here, it's like an elephant's
           been sick.

NICKY   Where?

MEL   Table four . . .

NICKY   Oh yeh . . . seafood pasta.

CAROL   My back's killing me . . .

MEL   Innit quiet . . .

CAROL   I've got neckache . . .

NICKY   Yeh it is.

CAROL   My feet are killing me . . .

NICKY   Somebody coming . . .

CAROL   (*noticing a member of the audience, a punter*) Sorry
           we're closed, closed, read my lips. If you can read.
           Closed.

NICKY   You should have come earlier.

CAROL   They're trying to get a last drink.

NICKY   It's because the lights are on.

CAROL   Closed sorry. No I can't sorry.

NICKY   They won't listen. Look at 'em, they're pissed up
           anyway.

           (MEL *walks to the spot.*)

CAROL   You tell 'em Mel, I'm shagged out.

NICKY   Carol.

CAROL   (*to audience*) Sorry.

MEL   Oi fuck off we're shut! (*To the others.*) They're
           going. I think they got the message.

(ADELE *who has been stood upstage, joins the others as the lights fade to night. The four stand as at the beginning.*)

ADELE   And then the long walk home. Your footsteps resound through the night. And you are alone in the dark. Alone in the night.

CAROL   All is dark, the pavestones are wet with the sweat of the night.

MEL   And as you walk, shadows in doorways, noises around corners. Coming towards you, two dark figures.

NICKY   Should you run. Oh God they're coming straight for you. You freeze to the spot.

ALL   Goodnight love . . . ha ha . . . d'you wanna come to a party . . .

CAROL   No.

ALL   No thanks.

CAROL   I've just been to one. We are Carol.

ADELE   Adele.

NICKY   Nicky.

MEL   And Mel.

ALL   And we work in a bar that is worse than hell.
We serve the drinks and we serve the food.
We have to be nice.
Not ever be rude,
So no matter what you do,
No matter what you say,
It's a happy smiling face . . .
That comes your way.

(*The actresses smile and freeze. Housemartin's "Happy Hour" plays. There is a slow fade to black.*)